I0540293

THIS BOOK BELONGS TO

_____

FOR THE KIDS WHO WANT TO
FIGHT FOR THE PEOPLE THEY LOVE

ISBN: 9798894581866

THE TOWN OF EVERNIGHT HADN'T SEEN SUNLIGHT IN WEEKS. SHADOWS STRETCHED ENDLESSLY, AND THE PEOPLE WHISPERED ABOUT A CURSE. THE MOON HUNG STILL, GLOWING PALE AND UNCHANGING ABOVE THEM.

LILA, A CURIOUS GIRL WITH AN ADVENTUROUS SPIRIT, STOOD OUTSIDE HER COTTAGE. SHE GAZED AT THE MOON, HER FINGERS BRUSHING THE MYSTERIOUS MEDALLION SHE'D FOUND IN THE WOODS DAYS BEFORE.

MAX, HER FEARLESS BEST FRIEND, SKIDDED TO A STOP BESIDE HER,
HIS SLINGSHOT DANGLING FROM HIS WRIST. "WHAT'S WRONG WITH THE SKY?
IT'S LIKE THE SUN FORGOT ABOUT US."

OWEN, THE CLEVER BOOKWORM OF THEIR TRIO, ARRIVED, CLUTCHING A DUSTY OLD TOME. "IT'S NOT JUST THE SKY. I FOUND SOMETHING IN MY GRANDFATHER'S LIBRARY ABOUT A SHADOW SORCERER."

OPENING THE BOOK, OWEN POINTED TO AN ILLUSTRATION OF A HOODED FIGURE SURROUNDED BY DARKNESS. "THE SHADOW SORCERER CONTROLS THE MOON. HE'S THE REASON THE SUN WON'T RISE!"

"THEN WE HAVE TO STOP HIM!" LILA EXCLAIMED, HER DETERMINATION SHINING BRIGHTER THAN THE MOON. SHE GRIPPED HER MEDALLION TIGHTLY. "WHERE IS HE?"

OWEN ADJUSTED HIS GLASSES AND FLIPPED THE PAGES.
"THERE'S A TOWER DEEP IN THE FOREST. BUT THE BOOK SAYS ONLY THE
BRAVE CAN FIND THE WAY."

MAX SMIRKED, LOADING A PEBBLE INTO HIS SLINGSHOT. "BRAVE?
THAT'S US. LET'S PACK SOME LANTERNS AND FIND THIS GUY."
LILA AND OWEN NODDED, READY FOR THE JOURNEY AHEAD.

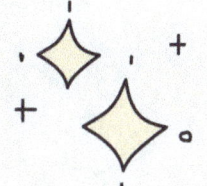

UNDER THE FAINT MOONLIGHT, THE TRIO STEPPED INTO THE EVERDARK WOODS. THE TREES LOOMED TALL AND TWISTED, THEIR SHADOWS CREATING EERIE SHAPES ON THE PATH.

STRANGE SOUNDS FILLED THE AIR—RUSTLING LEAVES, FAINT WHISPERS, AND DISTANT HOWLS. "STICK TOGETHER," LILA SAID FIRMLY, GRIPPING HER LANTERN TIGHTER AS THEY VENTURED DEEPER INTO THE SHADOWS.

SUDDENLY, MAX STOPPED, POINTING AHEAD. "LOOK AT THOSE CARVINGS ON THE TREES. THEY LOOK LIKE... RUNES?" OWEN STEPPED CLOSER, TRACING HIS FINGERS OVER THE SYMBOLS.

"IT SAYS, 'LIGHT REVEALS THE WAY,'" OWEN READ ALOUD.
MAX HELD UP THEIR LANTERN, AND A GLOWING TRAIL APPEARED,
WINDING DEEPER INTO THE FOREST.

THE GLOWING PATH LED THEM TO AN OLD, CREAKY BRIDGE HANGING OVER A RUSHING RIVER. THE WOODEN PLANKS SWAYED UNDER THEIR WEIGHT AS THEY STEPPED CAUTIOUSLY.

HALFWAY ACROSS, A SHADOWY CREATURE ROSE FROM THE DARKNESS BELOW.
ITS RED EYES GLOWED, AND IT GROWLED LOW, BLOCKING THEIR WAY.
"TURN BACK, OR FACE THE SHADOWS!"

MAX RAISED HIS SLINGSHOT, BUT LILA HELD UP HER MEDALLION. THE CREATURE HISSED
AND RECOILED, VANISHING INTO THE NIGHT.
"THE MEDALLION SCARED IT AWAY," OWEN WHISPERED, AWED.

ON THE OTHER SIDE OF THE BRIDGE, THEY FOUND A CLEARING WITH A STONE PEDESTAL IN ITS CENTER. THE PEDESTAL SHIMMERED FAINTLY IN THE MOONLIGHT, CARVED WITH INTRICATE PATTERNS.

OWEN KNELT TO READ THE INSCRIPTION. "WHAT BRINGS LIGHT BUT HAS NO SHADOW?" MAX FROWNED, AND LILA GASPED. "FIRE! QUICK, LIGHT THE TORCH!"

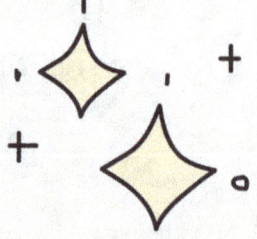

MAX STRUCK A MATCH, AND AS THE FLAME DANCED TO LIFE, THE PEDESTAL SLID OPEN, REVEALING A STAIRCASE DESCENDING INTO DARKNESS. "READY?" LILA ASKED. THEY NODDED.

THE STEPS TWISTED DOWNWARD, THE AIR GROWING COLDER WITH EACH TURN.
SHADOWS MOVED IN THE CORNERS OF THEIR EYES,
BUT WHEN THEY LOOKED, NOTHING WAS THERE.

AT THE BOTTOM, THEY FOUND A MASSIVE WOODEN DOOR CARVED WITH CRESCENT MOONS. IT GROANED OPEN TO REVEAL A CAVERN LIT BY FAINTLY GLOWING CRYSTALS.

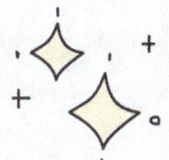

IN THE CAVERN'S CENTER LOOMED THE SHADOW SORCERER'S TOWER, TALL
AND FOREBODING. DARK MIST SWIRLED AROUND ITS BASE, WHISPERING
UNINTELLIGIBLE SECRETS. "WE'RE CLOSE," LILA SAID, HER VOICE STEADY.

INSIDE THE TOWER, THE AIR WAS HEAVY AND COLD. A SPIRALING STAIRCASE LED UPWARD, BUT EVERY STEP FELT AS IF UNSEEN EYES WERE WATCHING THEM FROM THE SHADOWS.

HALFWAY UP, A SHADOWY GUARDIAN EMERGED, BLOCKING THEIR PATH. ITS DEEP VOICE BOOMED, "ONLY THOSE WHO ANSWER MY RIDDLE MAY PASS. WHAT GROWS WHEN SHARED BUT SHRINKS WHEN HOARDED?"

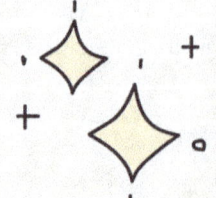

THE TRIO FROZE, THINKING. "A SECRET!" LILA EXCLAIMED. THE
GUARDIAN DISSOLVED INTO MIST, ALLOWING THEM TO CONTINUE.
MAX GRINNED. "NICE ONE, LILA."

AT THE TOP, THEY ENTERED A ROOM OF MIRRORS. EACH REFLECTION SHOWED
A TWISTED, SHADOWY VERSION OF THEMSELVES. "DON'T TRUST THE REFLECTIONS,"
OWEN WARNED, GRIPPING LILA'S ARM.

MAX NOTICED ONE MIRROR HAD NO REFLECTION. "THERE!" HE STEPPED THROUGH, AND THE OTHERS FOLLOWED INTO A DARK CHAMBER FILLED WITH SWIRLING SHADOWS.

AT THE CHAMBER'S CENTER STOOD THE SHADOW SORCERER HIMSELF,
CLOAKED IN DARKNESS. HIS GLOWING RED EYES PIERCED THROUGH THE GLOOM.
"SO, YOU'VE COME TO CHALLENGE ME," HE SNEERED.

LILA STEPPED FORWARD, GRIPPING HER MEDALLION. "WE'RE HERE TO STOP YOU. THE SUN BELONGS TO EVERYONE, NOT JUST YOUR SHADOWS!"

THE SORCERER LAUGHED COLDLY. "YOU'RE FOOLISH TO THINK YOU CAN DEFEAT ME. THE MOON IS MINE TO COMMAND, AND SOON, SO WILL THE STARS!"

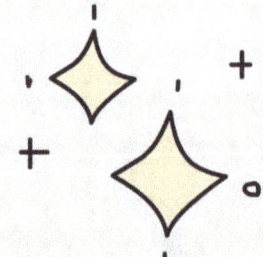

HE RAISED HIS STAFF, FILLING THE ROOM WITH SWIRLING SHADOW CREATURES.
MAX FIRED HIS SLINGSHOT, KNOCKING THE STAFF LOOSE,
BUT THE SORCERER'S POWER ONLY GREW STRONGER.

THE SHADOW SORCERER SUMMONED HIS SHADOW CREATURES TO ATTACK,
THEIR FORMS TWISTING AND SHIFTING LIKE SMOKE. "YOU'LL NEVER ESCAPE,"
HE SNARLED, HIS STAFF GLOWING OMINOUSLY.

MAX FIRED HIS SLINGSHOT, HITTING ONE SHADOW CREATURE, BUT IT REFORMED INSTANTLY. "THEY CAN'T BE HURT!" HE SHOUTED. LILA CLUTCHED HER MEDALLION TIGHTER, ITS LIGHT FLICKERING.

OWEN NOTICED THE GLOWING CRYSTALS ON THE WALLS. "THE CRYSTALS! THEY REFLECT LIGHT. WE CAN USE THEM!" HE SAID, PULLING LILA TOWARD ONE.

LILA HELD UP HER MEDALLION NEAR A CRYSTAL, AND THE LIGHT GREW STRONGER, PUSHING THE SHADOW CREATURES BACK. "IT'S WORKING!" SHE SAID AS THE CREATURES HISSED AND SHRANK.

THE SORCERER GROWLED. "YOU'RE CLEVER, BUT YOU'RE NO MATCH FOR THE DARKNESS." HE RAISED HIS STAFF, AND THE ROOM PLUNGED INTO DEEPER SHADOWS, SMOTHERING THE LIGHT.

THE KIDS STRUGGLED IN THE DARKNESS, UNABLE TO SEE EACH OTHER.
"DON'T LET GO OF THE MEDALLION!" MAX YELLED, HIS VOICE
BARELY AUDIBLE OVER THE SORCERER'S LAUGHTER.

LILA'S FINGERS TIGHTENED AROUND THE MEDALLION. "WE NEED MORE LIGHT!"
SHE CRIED, AND OWEN SHOUTED BACK, "THE MIRRORS FROM THE OTHER ROOM!
USE THE CRYSTALS WITH THE MIRRORS!"

THE TRIO SCRAMBLED, GATHERING CRYSTALS FROM THE WALLS AND HOLDING THEM TOWARD THE BROKEN MIRRORS. THE FAINT LIGHT FROM THE MEDALLION BEGAN TO MULTIPLY.

THE LIGHT GREW STRONGER, AND THE ROOM STARTED TO GLOW.
THE SHADOW CREATURES SCREECHED, DISSOLVING INTO THIN AIR.
THE SHADOW SORCERER'S RED EYES BURNED WITH FURY.

"NO! YOU WILL NOT DEFEAT ME!" HE ROARED, RAISING HIS STAFF AGAIN.
THE SHADOWS SURGED TOWARD THE CHILDREN ONE LAST TIME.

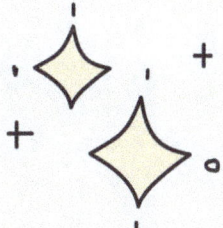

MAX LOADED HIS SLINGSHOT WITH A SHARP CRYSTAL SHARD AND FIRED.
IT HIT THE STAFF, CRACKING THE ORB AT ITS TIP. THE SORCERER SCREAMED IN RAGE.

LILA HELD THE MEDALLION HIGH, AND ITS LIGHT GREW BRIGHTER THAN EVER,
REFLECTING OFF EVERY CRYSTAL AND MIRROR IN THE ROOM.
THE COMBINED LIGHT ENGULFED THE SORCERER.

THE SORCERER'S SHADOWY FORM BEGAN TO FLICKER AND SHRINK.
"YOU... CAN'T... DEFEAT ME!" HE SCREAMED AS THE LIGHT BURNED AWAY
THE LAST OF HIS DARKNESS.

FINALLY, THE SHADOW SORCERER VANISHED, LEAVING ONLY
HIS SHATTERED STAFF BEHIND. THE ROOM FILLED WITH WARM LIGHT,
AND THE AIR FELT LIGHTER.

THE KIDS STOOD IN SILENCE FOR A MOMENT, CATCHING THEIR BREATH. "WE DID IT," LILA WHISPERED, HER VOICE FULL OF WONDER.

THE TOWER BEGAN TO TREMBLE, CRACKS FORMING ALONG THE WALLS.
"IT'S COLLAPSING!" OWEN SHOUTED. "WE HAVE TO GET OUT OF HERE!"

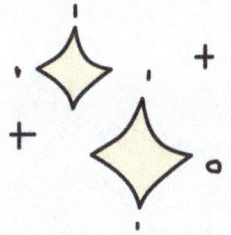

THE TRIO RAN DOWN THE SPIRALING STAIRCASE, DODGING FALLING DEBRIS. SHADOWS FLICKERED ON THE WALLS, BUT THEY FELT WEAK, FADING INTO NOTHINGNESS.

THEY REACHED THE CAVERN JUST AS THE TOWER COLLAPSED BEHIND THEM, THE GROUND SHAKING WITH A THUNDEROUS ROAR. "THAT WAS CLOSE," MAX SAID, GRINNING NERVOUSLY.

AS THE DUST SETTLED, A GOLDEN GLOW BEGAN TO SPREAD THROUGH THE CAVERN. THE MOON'S LIGHT SOFTENED, AND THE FIRST RAYS OF SUNLIGHT APPEARED AT THE HORIZON.

OUTSIDE THE FOREST, THE SUN ROSE FOR THE FIRST TIME IN WEEKS, BATHING THE TOWN OF EVERNIGHT IN WARM, GOLDEN LIGHT. THE PEOPLE EMERGED FROM THEIR HOMES, CHEERING.

THE TOWNSPEOPLE CHEERED, BUT THEIR RELIEF WAS SHORT-LIVED AS THE SKY DARKENED AGAIN. "WHAT'S HAPPENING?" A VILLAGER CRIED, POINTING AT THE CLOUDS SWIRLING OMINOUSLY.

THE KIDS NOTICED FAINT SHADOWS LINGERING IN THE FOREST.
"HE'S NOT COMPLETELY GONE," LILA SAID, CLUTCHING THE MEDALLION.
"WE NEED TO FINISH THIS."

OWEN EXAMINED THE BROKEN STAFF. "THE SOURCE OF HIS POWER MUST STILL BE OUT THERE. WE HAVE TO DESTROY IT COMPLETELY.

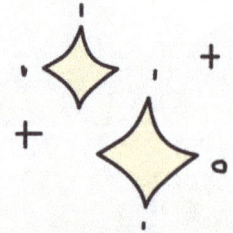

THE TRIO VENTURED BACK INTO THE WOODS, FOLLOWING THE
FAINT PULL OF DARKNESS. MAX GRIPPED HIS SLINGSHOT TIGHTLY,
READY FOR ANYTHING.

AS THEY APPROACHED THE RUINS OF THE TOWER, THE AIR GREW COLDER. THE SHADOWS COALESCED INTO A FIGURE—THE SHADOW SORCERER, WEAKER BUT STILL MENACING.

"YOU THINK YOU'VE WON?" HE SNEERED, HIS VOICE ECHOING. "
AS LONG AS SHADOWS EXIST, SO WILL I!"

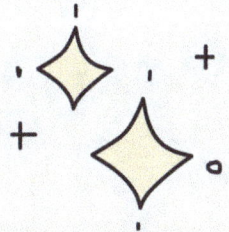

LILA HELD THE MEDALLION HIGH, ITS LIGHT FLICKERING AGAINST THE GROWING DARKNESS. "WE'LL STOP YOU ONCE AND FOR ALL!" SHE DECLARED.

THE SORCERER RAISED HIS BROKEN STAFF, AND THE SHADOWS SURGED
TOWARD THEM. MAX FIRED CRYSTAL SHARDS, BREAKING APART SMALLER SHADOWS.

LILA NOTICED A GLOWING CRYSTAL EMBEDDED IN THE RUINS.
"THAT'S IT! THAT'S HIS TRUE SOURCE OF POWER!" SHE SHOUTED, POINTING.

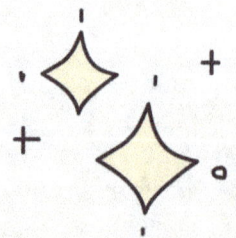

THE SORCERER BLOCKED THEIR PATH WITH A WALL OF DARKNESS. "YOU'LL NEVER REACH IT!" HE BELLOWED, HIS RED EYES BLAZING.

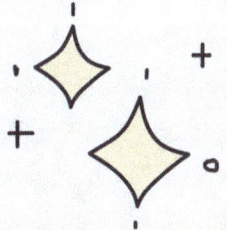

DRAINED BUT DETERMINED, LILA PUSHED FORWARD, THE MEDALLION'S LIGHT CARVING A PATH THROUGH THE DARKNESS. "WE CAN'T GIVE UP!"

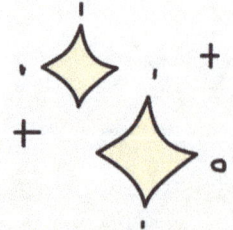

OWEN THREW HIS LANTERN, SMASHING IT AGAINST THE WALL OF SHADOWS. THE EXPLOSION OF LIGHT WEAKENED THE BARRIER, AND THEY PRESSED ON.

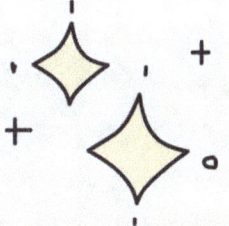

MAX AIMED HIS SLINGSHOT AT THE GLOWING CRYSTAL AND FIRED. THE SHOT CRACKED ITS SURFACE, SENDING A PULSE OF ENERGY THROUGH THE GROUND.

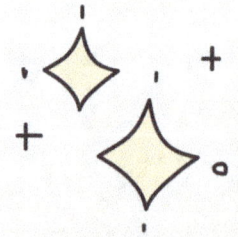

THE SORCERER SCREAMED AS HIS FORM FLICKERED, TRYING TO HOLD HIMSELF TOGETHER. "NO! YOU DON'T UNDERSTAND THE POWER YOU'RE UNLEASHING!"

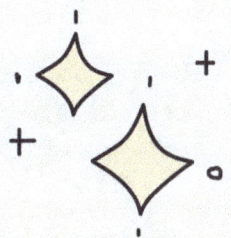

LILA STEPPED CLOSER, THE MEDALLION BLAZING. "THIS POWER BELONGS
TO THE LIGHT!" SHE TOUCHED THE CRYSTAL, AND IT
SHATTERED INTO A MILLION GLOWING SHARDS.

THE SORCERER LET OUT A FINAL, DEAFENING SCREAM AS THE LIGHT CONSUMED HIM. THE SHADOWS DISSOLVED, LEAVING ONLY SILENCE AND GOLDEN LIGHT.

THE FOREST BRIGHTENED, AND THE TOWER RUINS CRUMBLED COMPLETELY. LILA, MAX, AND OWEN STOOD TOGETHER, BATHED IN THE WARM SUNLIGHT.

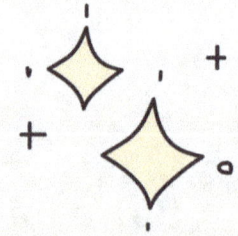

"IT'S OVER," OWEN SAID, BREATHING HEAVILY. "WE REALLY DID IT."
MAX GRINNED. "TOLD YOU WE COULD HANDLE IT."

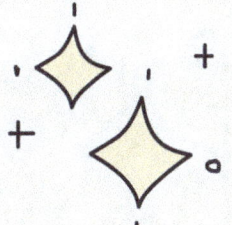

AS THEY WALKED BACK TO EVERNIGHT, THE VILLAGERS GREETED THEM WITH CHEERS AND HUGS. THE SUNLIGHT FELT WARMER THAN EVER BEFORE.

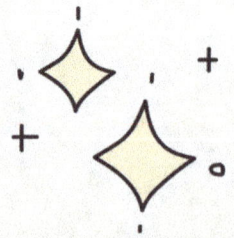

THE MEDALLION'S GLOW FADED, AND LILA PLACED IT IN THE TOWN FOUNTAIN.
"ITS WORK IS DONE," SHE SAID, SMILING.

THE TRIO SAT TOGETHER ON THE HILL, WATCHING THE SUNSET.
"THIS TOWN WILL NEVER FORGET WHAT WE DID," LILA SAID SOFTLY.

MAX STRETCHED OUT ON THE GRASS. "NEXT TIME, LET'S PICK AN EASIER ADVENTURE. MAYBE TREASURE HUNTING?"

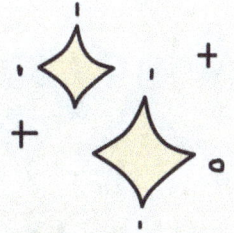

OWEN CHUCKLED, HOLDING UP HIS JOURNAL. "THIS STORY IS WORTH WRITING DOWN. PEOPLE NEED TO REMEMBER THE POWER OF COURAGE AND TEAMWORK."

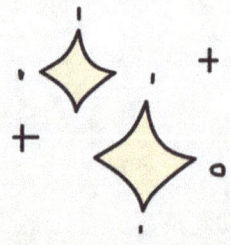

IN THE FOREST, THE TREES SWAYED GENTLY IN THE LIGHT. THE SHADOWS NO LONGER LOOMED, BUT THE MAGIC OF THE LAND FELT ALIVE AND PEACEFUL.

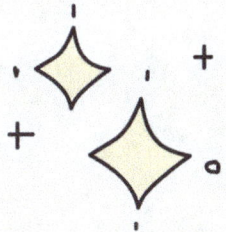

AND FAR AWAY, UNDER THE GOLDEN SKY, THREE BRAVE KIDS KNEW THEY HAD FOREVER CHANGED THEIR WORLD, BRINGING LIGHT WHERE THERE WAS ONCE ONLY DARKNESS.

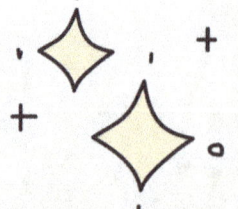

I HOPE YOU LIKED THE BOOK. BE SURE TO CHECK OUT MY OTHER BOOKS

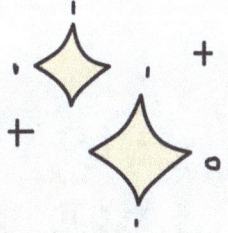

www.ingramcontent.com/pod-product-compliance
Lightning Source LLC
Chambersburg PA
CBHW081538120626
46550CB00009B/2788